THIS MOTHERING

Samantha Tucker

FOREWORD

Early motherhood and parenthood is a wholly wild and humbling experience; you are sleep-deprived, bewitched by the newness of this tiny person and continually astonished by how they change.

My two major vocations to date of endurance running and teaching teenagers about literature, turned out to be utterly useless and both easier than the unpredictability of this human raising.

I will always have the hugest respect to anyone who has raised children or parented in any capacity. I have an embodied awareness now of just how deep the well of love is and a clear knowledge of chronic sleep-deprivation when you don't have one of those unicorn babies that sleeps all night. Mine did not, until almost two years old.

In those early days, I am sure I oscillated between every emotion both low and high. Although at times I wanted to run far away, to any hotel that would have me and get a good night's sleep – I didn't. I stayed and walked through the fire and the madness and the sadness and the despair, and somewhere beyond it and in the middle of it was fierce love and pride along with moments of profound joy.

I am so grateful for the magic of creativity for letting me create, particularly in the absence of sleep. Nearly all of these poems came to me in the middle of the night, after many wake-ups to nurse my son. I would sit on the rocking chair with his warm body pressed against me as the clock said 9pm, 11pm, 1am, 3am, 4am… and my exhausted brain would somehow be conjuring up ideas to be scribbled down in an open Moleskine notebook. They appeared in the dark nights and gave me hope, inspiration fluttering on the peripheries to capture a little essence of this mothering.

Finally, this short collection is dedicated to my darling son, Toben, born in December of 2021. Thank you for making me a mother.

This Mothering   Samantha Tucker

Table of Contents

I Should Like to Be a Mother Someday..1
Trimester One...2
Mother Land: Day One...3
Never Leave Your Baby Unattended..5
Dreadlocks In Motherhood: Two Months..6
The Morning After a Bad Sleep..7
Night Crier..8
Matrescence: Four Months..9
Growing: Five Months..10
One Hundred and Fifty Five Days Old...11
Snot Box: Six Months...12
Sea Shell..13
Haikus: Seven Months..14
Polzeath...15
Heatwave...16
Nightcap For Motherhood...17
The Hostess of Motherhood..19
Today's Grid Reference: Eight Months..21
A Betrothal..22
Maternity Leave: 9.30pm..23
September's House: Nine Months..24
Border Supermarket..25
Holiday Haikus...26
Glitter Girl..27
Intruder: Eleven Months...28
First Autumn...30
Twelve Months of Parenting...31

iii

The Rules On Salt: Thirteen Months..32
This Mothering: Fourteen Months..33
Becoming My Mother...34
My Son..35

This Mothering   Samantha Tucker

I Should Like to Be a Mother Someday

I thought, but in that abstract way
As I cycled along side some beach:
Annagassan or Clogger Head
One hand pressed to my impossibly flat stomach
Feeling that solo adventurer's joy
Tent strapped to my bicycle,
Mac and cheese packets, a few carrots, berries
Sardines at the bottom of a pannier – just in case –
With the wind in my hair
And that knowledge of new places.
Would I ever feel life bloom in my stomach?

Trimester One

My intake was soupy yellow, creams and beige,
A fat moon cast across a plate.
We ate *Pom Bear* crisps and sliced potatoes,
From your seed shape you called out for more:

Croissants and fry ups, eggs please.
A pear chopped with korma sauce
Crunchy nut cornflakes,
Whole milk – but only twice.
Cold water, *never* tepid:
fruit smoothies, orange juice.

I couldn't drive thirty minutes without stopping for a snack,
you put your orders in:
Thai sticky rice and bleached tofu
eaten with one hand on the way home from the sea.
Sweet and sour sauce on toast, plain pasta.
A cold cheese quiche in the *Asda* car park,
Spilling crumbs onto my work clothes,
clutches of unmarked essays on the seat beside me.

Mother Land: Day One

On a ward round, the nurses bustle brightly.
They're already having a conversation with my uterus,
advising it to lie fallow a while, be a crop rotation.
"Welcome to day one: contraception."

On the field of my belly, above its sliced frontier,
My new foundling is hours old.
Eyes squeezed shut with star-fished fingers,
skin crinkled from too long in the bath.

They jab me with anticoagulants.
I'm bruised, pregnancy glow gone,
Layered in lilac bed sheets,
Answering question after question:

Has your milk come in?
Is he warm enough?
Do you feel confident holding your baby?

I cradle his tiny body, part faberge egg,
part wild animal, who I don't yet know –
And I am a regular herd animal
– Around me the hay of hospital pillows
And brightness, my water jug refilled –

As we trundle on the low plains of the red book
Charting not quite enough gained,
My little one staying small,
Oblivious to the milk brimming beneath him

This Mothering   Samantha Tucker

Snuffling in his yellow state
Demanding feeds every hour.
Unable to stay awake,

He reaches a hand out for familiar land
Towards the contours of my face,
And I squeeze back,
Whisper, *welcome.*

Never Leave Your Baby Unattended

The midwife said,
Ok I whispered, sotto voce,
So I wheeled my delicate cargo to the bathroom,
Inchoate, cluttered and slow,
A horse and cart in training
Turning an awkward five-point turn,
My baby swaddled in hospital lilac,
Me standing under the hot shower
Trying to keep the steam off the perspex crib
As it grew smeary, he dozed on
Sleepy yellow with jaundice.

Never leave your baby unattended.
I swallowed her words faithfully,
Breastfeeding on the loo,
Sleeping upright, straight as an arrow
For weeks after.
My mind a frazzled space,
My arms a course in how to be safe:
The c-hold, pillows stacked,
Elbows propped
Rigid at a table,
Feeling like a child being reproached;
(Not the adult I now was)
Say please and thank you,
Never leave your baby unattended.

Dreadlocks In Motherhood: Two Months

I could have dreadlocks in motherhood, easily.
Time has oozed her follicles together.
Everything is less than clean:
(my "*grubster*" delicious son with his dirty fingernails)
even my mind is matted,
the deep love and the exhaustion
folded in together.

I brushed my hair into submission once.
Those days are past;
replaced by knots that there isn't time to untangle.
How to love this hard and not fear life?

I could have dreadlocks in motherhood, easily.
Motherhood is a house of mirrors,
a dizzying, ghoulish funfair of parts.
We try to work out where we stand
as our reflections shift again and again.

The Morning After a Bad Sleep

The island of motherhood feels grumpy,
Its love is grumpy too.
I'm losing my mind, sometimes.
I get this pulsing behind the eyes
And want to scream, to break things,
To have someone else do this job, *please*.

All of the failures in my life are polished
And glint like shiny pennies,
Adding up to too many pounds.

Night Crier

He loves me,
He loves me not.

Like a seal being flung fish at
To do another trick:
His smiles are my bait,
Without them, I will sink.

With his tiny, round mouth,
He shouts a reedy call:
I am in splinters.

Does he not know I'm the mother bird
Scouring, searching for treasure?

Matrescence: Four Months

I am a mother,
Made of love and tears,
Water and milk.

Plump fingers tug at me.
When I unlatch him, milk brims
Over, splashing his cheeks
Like raindrops.

Growing: Five Months

I carried him easily at first,
Nourished from a seed
In the peat of my belly
Until he was rooted and bigger and
ready to be born.

Now I carry him in my arms, feeding
him books, kisses and milk.

He drinks newness with his globe eyes
stares around at each activity:
My pale body in the shower from his rocker seat,
The crash of the washing machine on its final spin cycle,
A newspaper that he quickly learns to rip,
Bashing the table with chubby arms,
Clutching at the balled paper.

I think about him as I swim lengths at my local pool:
One lap up, one back
Diving and cavorting through the water.
Will my son feel powerful here too?

I think about him as I run loops of the park:
His happy jam-red cheeks,
arms windmilling in his cot,
Learning how to take up space.

One Hundred and Fifty Five Days Old

I lift my son high above my head until
he is almost in the tree canopy.

I hold him up like the surgeons did moments
after digging him out of my belly.

I think of them as miners panning hopefully for gold
or an auctioneer calling:

"Who will take this lot?
tiny boy, 3152g, just born."

Snot Box: Six Months

I dream of our future
With water fights,
Me teaching you to say: I love you too.
But for now, you are sleeping,
Mouth ajar, full of cold
And you'll only sleep pressed against one of us.
Chubby arms flung across a chest,
Safe in this nest we made for you.

Sea Shell

Everything is edible
when you're six months old.
He tastes a shell, softly at first, then
grabs its bold curve.

Trying out a beach day,
From our living room.
I imagine rivers of blood
Scraped from his tiny tongue.

How many times have I left
The sea bleeding?
The gritty shoal lapping at my ankles,
angry scrapes sired by the sea.

Salt to garnish,
Blood and salt.
Don't drink it! I would say
Of sand licked into sliced skin.

We are the beach bled:
I would have told him about this, someday.
Be ready, but he gets there first,
clutching a bronzed shell

A striped rosette,
ribboned with red:
holding blood and fire in his hands.

Haikus: Seven Months

The hammock's wide swing,
Staring up at the June sky…
How to raise our son?

***

Do I love too hard?
Can there be another way?
Or just right for him?

***

Last year I grew our small son,
This year some raspberries?
Time moves all of us along.

***

This is his best thing:
(Not books or blocks or teddies)
Shaking a rattle.

***

When do we stop this?
He squeals with joy easily
At almost nothing.

Polzeath

We camped on the cliffs above Polzeath beach,
Taking it in turns to plunge into the cooking pot
Of the sea with its roiling waves and surfers.
One of us is always watching the baby.

This trip was not home to his first swim,
He grabbed fistfuls of sand instead
And sweated under the plastic greenhouse of the pram,
As the rain lashed sideways.

My Iphone drowned in a Cornish puddle,
The seafloor of the tent changing
Its precise screen into a deckchair of stripes.
I try to hold fuzzy memories of a smaller boy,
As thousands of photographs are wiped.

He crawls along the field, trailing mud.
Our pitch demarcated by a burn line, grass
blackened, he crosses it in seconds
Moving across the untamed swatch of green
Beyond the altar of what is ours.

We scroll the forecast hopefully,
Sipping on Merlot and fruity IPA,
Looking for sunnier days,
Which will come, almost certainly
As we turn back up the motorway.

Heatwave

Little one, it's hot.
You turned seven months in a heatwave,
The shocking heat,
Swept us up.
Sticky hours passed,
Everyone but us seemed to own a paddling pool,
We saw them on the front lawns
As we moved slowly along the streets:

Hard plastic shells,
Craters, tubs,
Inflatable pods
And us,
Crab like,
Clutching at each other,
Bare arms and sun-creamed feet,
Strapped to my middle,
branches reaching out from sling straps
For the sun.

We had no choice
But to go home panting,
Pulsing heat gleaming from the streets,
Casting the garden hose
Around us eagerly
As a peacock preens her feathers,
Stretching, wide open –
pink skin on show,
And us washed clean,
Nude against the sun's glow.

Nightcap For Motherhood

In time for last orders at the bar,
I order a shot of sleep.

My mouth presses against
The wide
rim of the tumbler,
Imagining milk and ovaltine, a cloud of
Dopamine.

Sleep is pricey and hot pink,
Fizzes on my tongue,
Languid,
sexy and rabid,
Pulsing to the music,
Shedding silk pyjamas,
Slingback Jimmy Choos.

I'd predicted muted tones,
But the playlist is splendid.
She is the last chance
Before
lights out.

When I see sleep in my mind,
She is muffled
Folded hospital corners.
But this one is a starched sheet
Cracked open

This Mothering   Samantha Tucker

A backless dress and a bronzed back,
Fiery disco-dancing,
The jolt of electricity
Popping between wires,
She is the snap of a crocodile clip,
Against soft skin

The molten fuzz of her shot
In my throat,
chilli powered – *the sleep special* –

are inline skates spinning along my hallway
A blue flame licked
Along the top of the mix,
a christmas pudding
Waiting for the fumes to burn out.

Sleep will soothe,
In a stroke along the shoulder blades,
A touch above the clavicle.
Settle into petal-licked dreams,
Rose and Violet Creams,

And a window left ajar.
The music turned low
Night, night darling,
As she slips away,
I'm just nipping back to the bar

The Hostess of Motherhood

She is a great hostess,
Showing me round the wings:
basement first,
The tour:

Great facilities, she boasts
But I notice the red around her eyes,
Salmon slithers
And the weary putt putt of her shoulders
When she lifts.

Is motherhood heavy? I want to ask,
But it seems too personal,
so nod and smile.
Motherhood is fast,
I steam and dig and breathe hard,
clip-clop beside her.

Motherhood has made a nest in my bones
She says, over her shoulder, without a groan.

I ask her when she last took a holiday,
she cackles:
And in the cavern of her mouth
I spot:
Late library book fines,
Gluten free pancakes on the kitchen floor,
Odd socks, stickers, velcro shoes.

This Mothering

Samantha Tucker

I see her heart doubled in size,
Bursting ripe,
A swollen strawberry behind her chest,
Rising from her sternum –
And I look on in alarm,
As she squeezes my arm.

In a bag-for-life by the door,
An alarm clock,
Two-man canoe,
Stilettos,
Triangular, beautiful shoes,
Licked with dust, all of it.

We don't use these so much, she chirps,
And in her back pocket,
a frequent-flyer card snapped in two
And the antlers of a plastic deer.
A wedding invite up on the fridge dated last year.

When she finally lifts her bonnet,
Dried flowers tumble out,
Lily of the valleys, in cream and white.
She is Persephone of Motherhood,
There is so much I don't know.

Today's Grid Reference: Eight Months

Adventures used to have an understandable end:
Mountains, the top.
Now I'm squashed against a cover-less duvet
On the nursery floor
Touching the painted mountains on the wall.

Our adventure for now, love,
Is the northern lights of the bedside lamp beaming,
The tinny mix of electric bird song,
Our small footsteps clattering
around this semi-detached in the suburbs.

I try to love it all,
Knowing that sometime the whipped peaks
Of mountains will be more than my milk –
The greens and greys and blues of this house
Will be replaced by us out there
Reaching for forest and sea and sky.

A Betrothal

Having a baby is a betrothal of sorts.
The slurry pit of learning and hoping.

Who will keep this child clean?
I will.

A crash course in love and wondering,
In preempting, what might go wrong.

Maternity Leave: 9.30pm

The light is so bright tonight.
Summer is underway,
This year everything is different.
The classroom of motherhood
I called it,
Emailing work to say,
Sorry I won't be back.
I hid the truth, that I couldn't leave him.

I sat on the back porch step
My nerves a jangle, on edge,
I used to be brave,
Now I question every feeling
And thought.
Perhaps in the future
is the woman I once was,
Only upgraded:
Tougher, stronger.

In the orange glow of sunset,
It is clear that there is so much love here.
This weary heart is full,
a sprawl of giving and then some.

September's House: Nine Months

Was on the road,
Sticky with apricot jam
And the salvaged ends of baguettes.
We toasted everything:

The sharp V-neck of the mountains
As they interlocked fingers,
Horn rimmed elders in the sky,

Us parked in the dry river bed,
The sprinter van's wheels on ancient stones.

The start of Christmas trees rising
Around us, pine scented growing

our unwashed babe, crawling
Beyond the tartan picnic rug.

We toasted everything:
His nine months of exploring.

We were asked: *Que tiempo años hace?*
How much time has he made?

Border Supermarket

French and Spanish spoken
But no baby food.
Me unrolling my yoga mat
Under the floodlights
Of the *Super U*
Jute pressing into gravel:
Cowbells ringing out,
Carrier bags full of white-beans,
Rioja wine and nougat.

Holiday Haikus

Campsite by the sea
A trainline in the distance
Sliver of crescent
Moon, fishermen haul their lines

***

Out of season
September in Northern Spain
Breeze moves the palm trees
Back home we know it's raining

***

Swimming
Gulping at the salty sea
Breathing in the sun
9 months old; so much newness

***

A moving house
How many cups of tea drunk?
A feeling of home
Everywhere we park the van

Glitter Girl

My aunt used to wear
this eyeshadow pot in the 90's,
Urban Decay in midnight grey.

For weeks after a visit,
I'd spot a dot of her glitter:
Now flashing on my son's face.

At night when we wake to feed
I imagine us shimmering in the dark.
Silver splashed, and others elsewhere,

bobbing away, flecked with light,
Urban Decay in midnight grey,
tending to our young.

Intruder: Eleven Months

Motherhood has dropped her hat
In my soup – it's the third time this week.
She chooses indiscriminately:
Heinz tomato,
Mulligatawny,
Leek and potato.
Short of flinging my spoon out,
Clattering into the sink,
I try again, less kindly:
Motherhood, this is my soup.
No sitting at this table, back off!
Didn't you learn any manners?

Later, I find out she's not
Taken her shoes off either,
Stomping old mud and leaves
Into the carpet of our bedroom,
The place with the bamboo sheets:
It's a step too far.

Here's the laundry bill,
I want to say,
But I know better;
She's not finished yet.

She's got the keys cut already,
(£10 for three at Timpsons)
Put a picture up in the hall,
Something saccharine:
A day at the zoo.

This Mothering   Samantha Tucker

I look closer,
She's planted orchids,
Put up extra shelves
filled my freezer with tiny pots.

Alright motherhood, I finally relent,
You can come in.

First Autumn

I lost track of time as we swept up leaves,
Waiting for rain water to soup our finds
As I broomed them together – tarmac black
Treacle, the clung to, stuck to, sodden bits,
caramel slithers, burnt orange, biscuit.
Roaring around us in the autumn wind,
a standing ovation. The sky fierce blue,
carrying the evening towards us.
My son's tiny fingers pinked with the cold,
And only this time last year, we dreamed him
As the world wrapped up for Christmas again,
buoyant in the clasps of my warm belly,
waiting to be born. I pounded the streets,
with a thick coat, holding on and hoping.

This Mothering — Samantha Tucker

Twelve Months of Parenting

I wish we could fall in love, again,
Unpick what made us work
– like scraping snow from my car windscreen –
In that sudden December cold snap
When you scratched into the frosting
That you loved me. I drove away,
Accelerating into the first light
Of morning with our small son,
Already asleep in his car seat.

At home these days,
weaving between rooms
He learns to walk in colt-like staggers.
One foot padding
After the other, again,
Impatient to be at our level, upright.

We scoop up toys as we go,
"Found it" I call,
Beneath the coffee table,
in the fruit bowl nestled by oranges,
Behind the fridge,
Games of peekaboo,
Holding this or that –
A tiny brick or a chopstick.
I reach back into these hidden-away spaces,
Hunting amidst the plastic balls
And the story books and clutter:
Mostly triumphant,
hoping for a way back to you.

The Rules On Salt: Thirteen Months

I haven't put the TV on yet,
It's my wildcard and I'm saving it.
But I've broken the rules on salt.

His joy in marmite pasta
Was a dolphin breaking
through a wave
all nose, rocking happily up and down
In the grey sea of the high chair.

He claps when he wakes up,
I love how he delights in morning:
another one!

We cook together and bake and make,
hurling celery chunks
And kiwis into the juicer,

Weighing and measuring on the steel scales
As I hold tight each gram,
these fragments.

This Mothering: Fourteen Months

Prising open the nursery drawers,
I turn clothes the right way.
They're often inside out,
these little trousers – the first denim jeans –
Lion socks, Paddington sweater,
Pulled off my son and swapped for a sleep suit.

My heart – jellied and doubled –
When carrying my son,
Pumping more blood around for us both,
edges ready to burst their dams,
To coo a soft word, murmur love,
To encourage.

I was a mother in waiting,
An ancestral line tugging me along,

I carry it forwards,
This mothering,
Even when days feel inside out,
Chaotic, charged,
I carry it forwards, this fire,
Full bodied, ancient:
Light a candle for bedtime.

I carry it forwards, this fire,
Carve the sacred into the small things,
Light a candle for bedtime.

Becoming My Mother

In joining motherhood,
I didn't realise I'd become my own mother.
Stepping into her patent Gabor flats:
Leaving the water running
As I soap and scrub the dinner plates,
Hurrying
The fish cutlery, the empty jars and lids,
That worry would hold me in its vice grip,
Strong and haughty,
That I'd be a held woman,
Committed to the house of the what-ifs,
To the outrageous, over-the-top love for my child.

My Son

Planting a tree you'll never see,
Saying to the great blank pages of the future
I believe in you.

Having a child: sweet pea
Sugar plum, little bunny
Because mine – in his elephant print pyjamas –

Is hopeful
And just briefly I can forget my place in the world
– The great gleaming globe –

And swim in the thought of him.
When he drops his head back to laugh I see
a fisherman casting his net out,

When he presses my lips with his wide-open fingers
And my freckles as if they'll disappear,
I know he can tell me things already.

Look up mama,
He seems to be saying,
Look up and see it all.

Printed in Great Britain
by Amazon